RADIO ASTRONOMY

PUBLISHED BY SMART APPLE MEDIA

123 SOUTH BROAD STREET

MANKATO, MINNESOTA 56001

PHOTOS: PAGE 7—JASON WARE; PAGE 8—CORBIS/BETTMANN;

PAGE 11—NASA; PAGES 13, 14, 19, 30—NATIONAL RADIO ASTRONOMY

OBSERVATORY; PAGE 15—COURTESY OF NAIC—ARECIBO OBSERVATORY,

A FACILITY OF THE NSF (PHOTOS BY TONY ACEVEDO); PAGES 23, 25, 27—

NASA/JPL/CALTECH; PAGE 29—IAC PHOTO MADE FROM PLATES TAKEN

WITH THE ISAAC NEWTON TELESCOPE BY DAVID MALIN

DESIGN AND PRODUCTION: EVANSDAY DESIGN

LIBRARY OF CONGRESS CATALOGING-IN-PUBLICATION DATA

RICHARDSON, ADELE, 1966–

RADIO ASTRONOMY / BY ADELE D. RICHARDSON

P. CM. — (ABOVE AND BEYOND)

INCLUDES INDEX.

SUMMARY: EXAMINES THE SCIENCE OF RADIO ASTRONOMY

SINCE ITS DISCOVERY IN 1932.

ISBN 1-58340-051-6

1. RADIO ASTRONOMY—JUVENILE LITERATURE. [1. RADIO ASTRONOMY.]

I. TITLE. II. SERIES: ABOVE AND BEYOND (MANKATO, MINN.)

QB478.R53   1999

522'.682—DC21   98-20890

FIRST EDITION

1 3 5 7 9 8 6 4 2

RADIO ASTRONOMY

ADELE D. RICHARDSON

ABOVE & BEYOND

SLOWLY AND METHODICALLY, the huge dish turned on its base, its long antenna jutting toward the sky ✳ Nearby, a radio astronomer patiently listened through headphones ✳ Suddenly, a clear signal rang out ✳ Computers came alive to process the discovery, and printers spat out page after page of information ✳ Something new had emerged out in deep space: perhaps a new star, a whole new galaxy, or even life on another planet ✳ Whatever the source, its constant pattern of radio waves could not—and would not—be ignored ✳

Listening to the Stars

The man responsible for the start of **radio astronomy** in 1932 was not even an astronomer. Karl Jansky was a radio engineer employed by Bell Telephone Laboratories in New Jersey. Jansky's job was to identify the crackling static that interfered with some shortwave telephone communications, such as calls from ships to shore.

To "listen" to this static, Jansky built a huge radio antenna out of lumber and wires. By the time he was finished, the antenna resembled a merry-go-round the size of a house. Wheels from a Model-T Ford allowed Jansky to move his invention from place to place.

After a few early experiments, Jansky found that most of the static came from thunderstorms, airplanes, and other common sources in Earth's atmosphere. But he also heard a soft static in the background. Thinking it might be the sun, Jansky pointed his antenna toward the glowing orb. But the sun wasn't the source. On an impulse, he angled the antenna toward the openness of outer space and started listening.

By accident, Jansky had founded a whole new science: radio astronomy. He later determined that the background static originated at the center of our Milky Way

Galaxy. Although his findings appeared on the front page of the *New York Times* on May 5, 1933, professional astronomers didn't take much interest in Jansky's discovery. To them, it was little more than a curiosity. Only Grote Reber, a radio engineer from Wheaton, Illinois, decided to study this static from outer space.

When Reber heard about Jansky's discovery, he realized that listening to radio waves was a whole new way to

The M-31 Andromeda Galaxy, shown here, looks much the same as our own Milky Way Galaxy.

Radio astronomy *is the science of using radio waves to study objects in space.*

explore the heavens. In 1937, he decided to build an instrument that would let him listen to the stars. It took him four months and $4,000 of his own money to do it, but when he was finished, Reber had created the world's first **radio telescope** in his own backyard.

The most impressive part of Reber's creation was a **parabolic dish** antenna that was 32 feet (9.8 m) across. This dish, also called a reflector, collected radio waves from space. These waves were then reflected to a point at the front of the dish, where a large receiving antenna picked them up. Reber added an amplifier to make the static louder, and he tracked the noise on a graph.

Reber began matching objects detected by his radio telescope with the objects shown on an astronomical map of the universe. This map had been created by as-

*A **radio telescope** is an instrument used to transmit or listen to radio signals.*

*A **parabolic dish** is the bowl-shaped antenna or reflector of a radio telescope.*

Karl Jansky, the founder of radio astronomy.

tronomers using regular optical telescopes. As Reber found new objects, he added them to the map, creating the first radio map of the universe. For several years, he was the world's only radio astronomer.

After World War II, many countries began experimenting with **radar** technology. Using the same structure as Reber's telescope, radar equipment sent radio waves into the air. When the waves struck an object, they would return to the antenna, indicating the size of the object and its distance from the dish. Although radar was initially developed for military applications, its usefulness in the field of radio astronomy quickly became apparent. This technology was responsible for much of the early progress in radio observation of space.

Radar *is a system that uses radio waves to gather information on distant objects.*

Enormous and powerful telescope antennas allow us to listen to the far reaches of the universe.

Radio Telescopes

Karl Jansky's discovery of radio waves in space advanced the entire field of astronomy. Scientists who use optical telescopes can study only the visible portion of the **electromagnetic spectrum**. The visible spectrum includes seven colors: red, orange, yellow, green, blue, indigo, and violet. Each color has its own **wavelength**, ranging from violet, which has the shortest wavelength, to red, which has the longest. As a group, the colors in this spectrum are called visible light.

Visible light is just a small part of the electromagnetic spectrum, which includes all of the electrical and magnetic waves in our universe. Visible light is near the middle of the spectrum. Just below the red wavelength of visible light is a range of longer wavelengths called infrared light. The heat from the sun falls into this category. Although we can't see infrared light, it is critical to support life; without it, the planets in our solar system would be mere balls of ice.

Toward the other end of the spectrum, above the violet wavelength, is a range of wavelengths called ultraviolet light. Unlike infrared, ultraviolet light does not give off heat. However, ultraviolet rays emitted by the sun are re-

The **electromagnetic spectrum** *is a range of wavelengths.*

sponsible for the sunburn people get on sunny days. Ultraviolet light is also the part of the spectrum that allows certain objects to glow in the dark.

The electromagnetic spectrum also includes X rays, microwaves, and **gamma rays**. Many of these invisible but dangerous waves are blocked by Earth's atmosphere before they reach the planet's surface. However, scientists are concerned about the growing effect of these harmful waves on people; as the ozone layer is weakened by man-made chemical compounds called fluorocarbons, more and more of these waves reach Earth.

Radio waves are the long waves at the farthest end of the electromagnetic spectrum, below infrared light. Television and radio stations use radio waves to broadcast

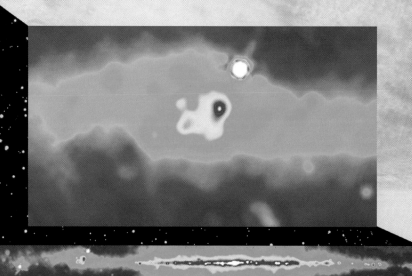

An image of the spectrum of radio waves from the Milky Way Galaxy (bottom), with a section magnified (top).

A **wavelength** *is the distance from one peak to the next in any kind of wave movement.*

Gamma rays *are the most energetic and deadly rays in the electromagnetic spectrum.*

their programs. These are also the waves that radio astronomers use to study the universe.

Grote Reber's radio telescope showed astronomers how to overcome some of the limitations of optical telescopes. Traditional telescopes function poorly in daylight, and pollution and the earth's atmosphere can obscure the view through their lenses, preventing astronomers from getting a clear picture of space. These factors, however, do not interfere with the operation of radio telescopes.

Radio telescopes can also send radio signals into space and bounce them off of distant objects. In fact, much of what astronomers know about comets has been learned by bouncing signals off of comets' tails. This technique has also enabled astronomers to map the side of the moon that faces the earth.

Since Reber built his backyard antenna more than 60 years ago, scientists have constructed radio telescopes throughout the world. One of the earliest radio telescope systems, called the Mills Cross, was invented in 1953. This system, which is no longer built today, used two long antennas angled toward the sky at right angles to one another. Signals collected by the two antennas were then multiplied together to create a single signal. The largest Mills Cross, built in Australia, has antennas that are each one mile (1.7 km) long.

Images of a radio telescope being constructed in Greenbank, West Virginia.

Workers completed the first giant radio telescope in 1957 in Jodrell Bank, England. The telescope, called the Mark 1A, took six years to build and was partially constructed out of pieces of old battleships. Its dish, measuring 250 feet (76 m) across, is movable, so astronomers can position it exactly where they want it. Mark 1A made history in 1957 by tracking the first Russian satellite, *Sputnik 1*, as it orbited the earth.

The world's largest radio telescope is located in the jungles of Puerto Rico, near the town of Arecibo. The dish, completed in 1963, sits in an enormous natural limestone bowl that is 1,000 feet (305 m) in diameter. Because this gigantic dish was built into the ground, scientists cannot move the telescope. However, it has transmitting equipment and a movable antenna that hangs from massive cables, allowing scientists to direct its radio signals into space. The whole package, including the dish, antenna, cables, and three concrete towers, weighs about 600 tons (546 t). The Arecibo telescope is so powerful that it has produced the most accurate map of Venus to date.

The impressive Arecibo radio telescope.

Strong towers and heavy cables are needed to move the Arecibo antenna.

Finding
a Signal

Radio astronomers soon discovered that bigger dishes produce clearer pictures. This discovery led to **radio interferometry**, a technique in which two or more radio telescopes are connected with cables. The combined telescopes then have the power of one huge telescope, giving astronomers an even more powerful way to explore the heavens.

Two of the most impressive radio interferometry systems in the world are in the United States. The first of the two systems, built in 1980 in New Mexico, is called the Very Large Array (VLA). This system consists of 27 separate dishes placed in a *Y* shape. Each arm of the *Y* includes nine movable dishes, and each dish is 82 feet (25 m) across. The antennas are near a railroad line, so astronomers can move them by rail. VLA antennas can be spread over an area more than 20 miles (32 km) wide. To match the power of the VLA, a single radio telescope dish would have to be 17 miles (27 km) in diameter.

Computers are an important part of interferometry systems. Each antenna receives its information at a slightly

The dishes that make up the Very Large Array are constantly listening for signals.

Radio interferometry is a technique in which cables connect two or more radio telescopes.

different time and from a slightly different location. Computers can take all of the incoming signals and blend them to provide scientists with complete and accurate information. This process works much like the human brain. If a person looks at an object with one eye at a time, the object is seen from two different angles. But if the person looks at the object with both eyes at once, the human brain blends the two images into one. If it weren't for computers, the information gathered through radio interferometry would be impossible to understand.

The second interferometry system in the U.S. is the Very Long Baseline Array (VLBA), completed in 1993. This system combines radio antennas that are hundreds of miles apart into one massive radio telescope. The VLBA consists of 10 parabolic dishes, each one 82 feet (25 m) in diameter. Scientists have placed the dishes across the U.S. and its territories, from Hawaii to the Virgin Islands; together, the dishes cover an area more than 5,000 miles (8,050 km) wide. The dishes are linked by computer, and

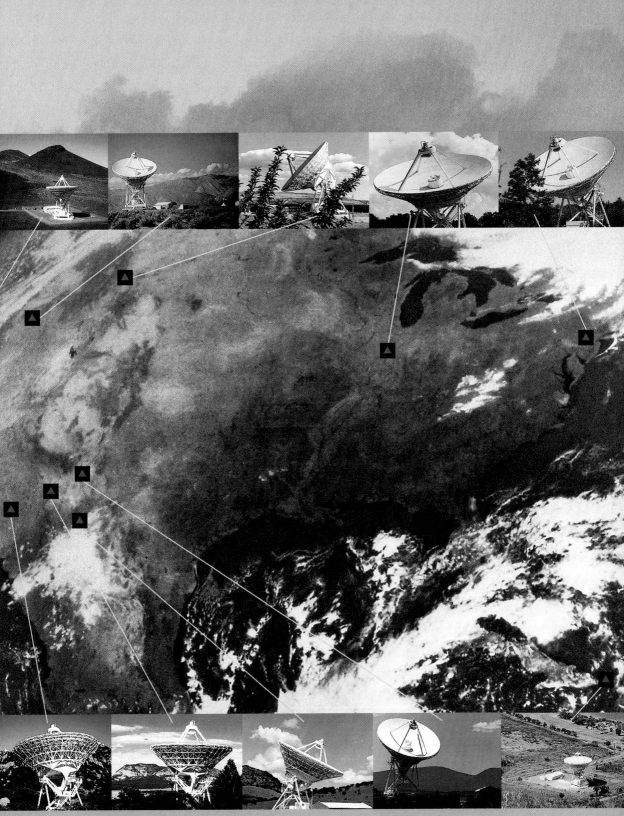

A map showing the widespread locations of the 10 dishes in the Very Long Baseline Array.

scientists transfer information from the telescopes over the Internet. The VLBA requires a very accurate kind of clock called the hydrogen maser system, which synchronizes—or coordinates together—the incoming signals from each radio antenna.

Radio astronomers have set up another VLBA in Europe. This array consists of the Jodrell Bank telescope linked with a 320-foot (100 m) dish in West Germany and 14 other dishes in Holland.

Another breakthrough in radio astronomy was realized in February 1997, when Japan launched the *Highly Advanced Laboratory for Communications and Astronomy (HALCA)*, the first satellite designed specifically for radio astronomy. Astronomers around the world could one day connect to the satellite, in effect creating an Earth-sized radio telescope.

Scientists could make an even bigger and more powerful radio telescope by placing a dish on the moon. If this is one day accomplished, radio astronomers will be able to explore the universe with a telescope that is hundreds of thousands of miles wide.

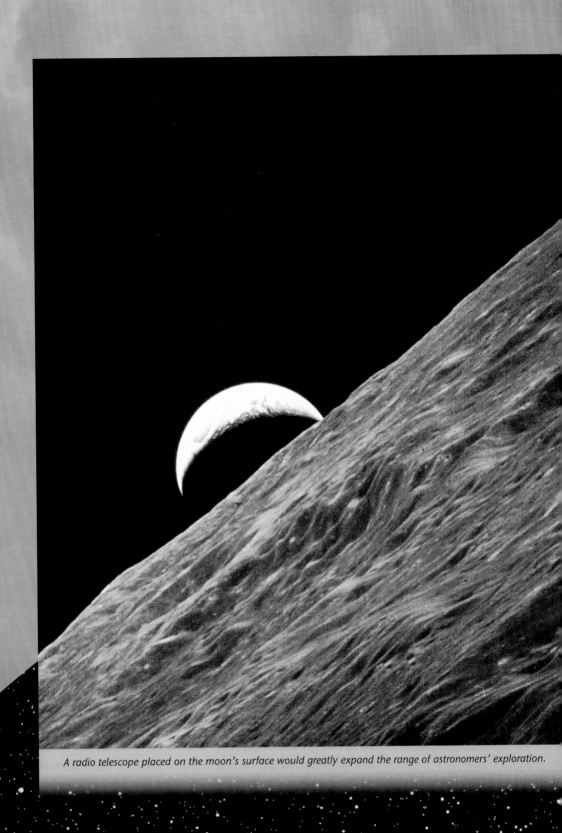

A radio telescope placed on the moon's surface would greatly expand the range of astronomers' exploration.

Exploring the Universe

Radio astronomers have made many major discoveries about our universe. In 1960, for example, two scientists were using an optical telescope to view what they thought was an ordinary star in our galaxy. When scientists looked at the same star with a radio telescope, however, they discovered that the star was bursting with radio wave activity. Intrigued, they looked at it again with a **spectroscope**.

The star did not act like normal stars, which do not give off so many radio waves. Scientists ultimately decided that, although this object resembled a star, it was something else entirely. They named this star-like celestial body a **quasi-stellar object**. Later, the name was shortened to "quasar." Astronomers have learned that quasars are the brightest objects in the universe.

In 1967, British radio astronomers discovered stars that "pulse," or send out bursts of radio signals at regular intervals. These stars were different from quasars, and most of them were not visible with an optical telescope. Rather than giving off continuous signals, they produced short

A **spectroscope** *is an instrument used to identify an object's composition and speed of travel.*

Images of quasars captured by the Hubble Space Telescope.

A **quasi-stellar object (quasar)** *is a star-like object that produces a lot of radio waves.*

bursts that lasted about one-twentieth of a second. By 1980, radio astronomers had located more than 300 of these pulsing stars, called **pulsars**.

Astronomers have learned that these pulsars are often the result of stars that have exploded. These enormous explosions, called **supernovas**, give off every kind of electromagnetic wave. A supernova may produce more energy in a few days than the sun does in 100 million years.

The most important pulsar astronomers have ever found is in the remains of a star that exploded in the year 1054. The supernova, which took place many trillions of miles from Earth, was so bright that it could be seen by the naked eye for three weeks in daylight and for two

*A **pulsar** is a spinning star that sends out bursts of radio signals.*

*A **supernova** is the highly energetic explosion of a large star.*

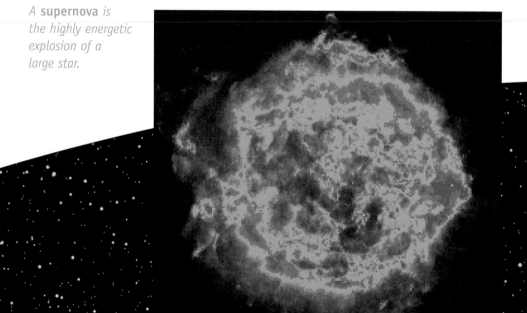

A supernova as seen through the Very Large Array.

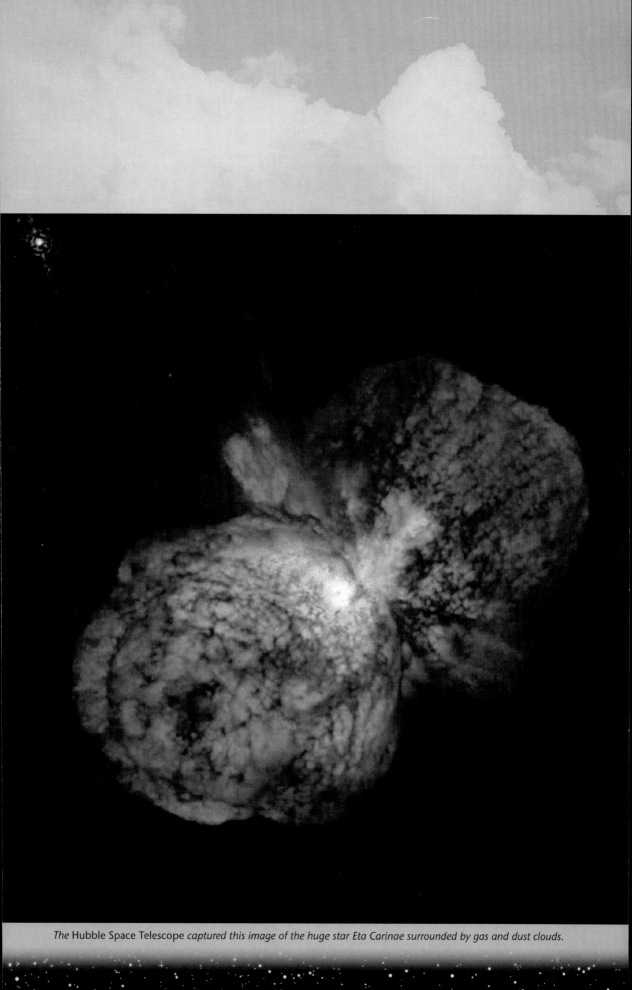

The Hubble Space Telescope *captured this image of the huge star Eta Carinae surrounded by gas and dust clouds.*

years at night. Even today, the explosion continues to expand outward thousands of miles every day.

Another interesting area of space study was born when astronomers began to examine the death of stars. Using the known laws of physics, scientists theorized that stars with a mass greater than that of the sun would die in one of two ways. Some stars would turn into dwarfs, dying stars that slowly lose their brilliance. Other stars would have their outer layers blown off in a supernova, leaving only a small center called a neutron star.

Scientists believed that smaller stars would die differently. According to their theory, such a star's gravitational pull would become so great that the star would literally be crushed into a smaller size. As the star collapsed, the force of its gravity would equal the speed of light, meaning that even light would be unable to leave the star's

A black hole is a former star that has been crushed by extreme gravity.

surface. The result would be a dense, black star. Scientists call such an object a **black hole**.

Radio astronomers believed that if black holes existed, the objects being drawn to their surfaces would send out X rays. Astronomers also believed that they would be able to detect these X rays with their radio telescopes. In 1971, scientists sent a special X ray-detecting telescope into orbit aboard a satellite. The telescope found what appeared to be a black hole far from Earth in the constellation Cygnus.

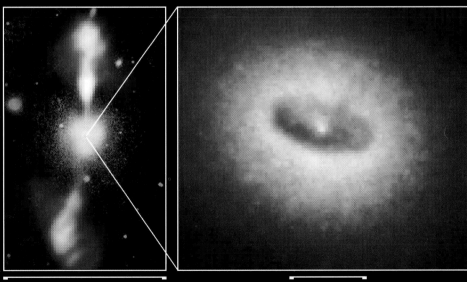

GROUND-BASED
OPTICAL/RADIO IMAGE

HST IMAGE OF A GAS AND DUST DISK

380 ARC SECONDS
88,000 LIGHTYEARS

17 ARC SECONDS
400 LIGHTYEARS

Radio astronomy has allowed us to see the accretion—energy produced by colliding space objects—surrounding black holes; the lightyears given represent the distance shown left to right in each image.

An Expanding World

Both radio and optical telescopes are windows to the past. Light and radio waves travel at a speed of 186,300 miles (300,000 km) per second. Sunlight can cover the distance from the sun to the earth in a little more than eight minutes. This means that a person who quickly glances at the sun is seeing what happened there about eight minutes earlier.

Other than the sun, the star nearest to Earth is Alpha Centauri, which is about four **light-years** from our planet. Light travels about 5.8 trillion miles (9.3 trillion km) in one year, so the nearest star is roughly 23 trillion miles (36.8 trillion km) away. Astronomers who study Alpha Centauri with a telescope are, in a sense, traveling back in time; they are seeing what happened four years in the past. If an explosion would ever happen on Alpha Centauri, scientists wouldn't find out about it until four years later.

Radio astronomers have also explored the universe using spectroscopes together with radio telescopes. Spectroscopes are used to identify the composition of objects and to determine how fast the objects are traveling. In the 1960s, scientists located a dim star more than two billion

This galaxy, called the M-33 Galaxy, is one of many studied with radio telescopes.

light-years away. This was exciting enough, but they also learned that the star was speeding away from our galaxy at more than 27,000 miles (43,450 km) per second. This discovery was the first indication scientists had found that our universe is expanding.

Astronomers soon located other objects that are also racing away from Earth. They found one quasar more

A **light-year** *is the distance light travels in one year.*

than four billion light-years away that was speeding away from us at the incredible rate of more than 50,000 miles (80,500 km) per second.

Perhaps radio astronomers' most intriguing area of work is the Search for Extraterrestrial Intelligence (SETI). The first real radio search for life beyond our solar system began in 1960 with a program called Project Ozma, which focused on two distant stars. In the years since this project, SETI astronomers throughout the world have continued to search the heavens for signs of life on other planets.

One SETI program, begun at a Harvard University observatory in 1983, uses an 84-foot (25.6 m) radio telescope to search for signals from about 68 percent of the sky. The National Aeronautics and Space Administration (NASA) started

The SETI program's original radio telescope.

another SETI program called the Microwave Observing Project in 1992. One part of the program studies about 1,000 sun-like stars, while another part involves scanning the entire sky.

So far, no beings have answered the SETI signals beamed into space. However, whether or not radio astronomers someday locate other intelligent beings in the universe, radio astronomy will continue to play a major role in our exploration of space. What began as one man's wooden invention in 1932 has grown into a complex and powerful means of mapping our universe. Long into the new millennium, radio astronomers will be listening to the stars.

Radio astronomers will continue to search the heavens for signs of extraterrestrial life.

INDEX

A
Alpha Centauri 28
Arecibo telescope 14, 15

B
Bell Telephone Laboratories 6
black holes 18, 26, 27

C
Cygnus 27

D
dwarf stars 26

E
electromagnetic spectrum 10, 11
Eta Carinae 25

G
Galileo 24
gamma rays 11, 26

H
Harvard University 30
*Highly Advanced Laboratory for
    Communications and As-
    tronomy (HALCA)* 20
hydrogen maser system 20

J
Jansky, Karl 6–7, 8, 10
Jupiter 24

L
light
    infrared 10
    ultraviolet 10–11
    visible 10

M
M-31 Andromeda Galaxy 7
M-33 Galaxy 29
Mark 1A 13, 20
microquasars 20
Microwave Observing Project 31
microwaves 11
Milky Way 6–7, 11
Mills Cross 12
moon 12, 21

N
National Aeronautics and Space
    Administration (NASA) 30
neutron stars 26
New York Times 7

O
ozone layer 11

P
parabolic dish 8
Project Ozma 30
pulsars 22–24

Q
quasars 12, 20, 22, 23, 29–30

R
radar 9
radio interferometry 16–20
radio map 8–9
radio telescope 8, 9, 12–14
Reber, Grote 7–9, 12

S
Search for Extraterrestrial Intelli-
    gence (SETI) 30–31
spectroscopes 22, 23, 28–29
Sputnik 1 13
supernovas 24, 26

V
Venus 14
Very Large Array (VLA) 16, 17, 24
Very Long Baseline Array (VLBA)
    18–20

X
X rays 11, 27